THIS IS
HOW WE
BEGIN

THIS IS
HOW WE
BEGIN

Devotionals
and Prayers
to Start Meetings

OPEN WATERS
PUBLISHING

Open Waters Publishing
700 Prospect Avenue
Cleveland, Ohio 44115
www.openwaterspublishing.com

Cover design by Ted Dawson Studio.

Printed in the United States of America

First Edition: October 2013

10 9 8 7 6 5 4 3 2 1

Open Waters Publishing is an imprint of The Pilgrim Press.
The Open Waters Publishing name and logo are trademarks
of Local Church Ministries, the United Church of Christ.

ISBN 978-08298-1995-3

CONTENTS

GROUP DYNAMICS

DECISIONS

BURNOUT

WHY DO WE DO THIS?

Extend a welcome to God, who is tired of being ignored at your church meetings.

Introduction

As one of our church boards welcomed new members, the board chair said, "This is how we begin, with prayer and a reflection on Scripture. It reminds us who we are—the church—and whose we are—sons and daughters of God and disciples of Jesus."

A simple and gracious statement, and an important one.

- We begin by remembering.
- We begin by pausing to become fully present to God and to one another.
- We begin by reminding ourselves that we are not so much "beginning" as "joining." We are joining a long and lively tradition of faith and practice.

Even as our words of prayer and reflection begin a meeting, there is a sense in which they are always the second word. The first word is God's.

How often do we run from a frantic day with our minds moving in a million directions, approaching church business or worship, or planning for service to others in God's name, and treat it like just one more thing on our to-do list?

How dare we?

Stop.

Breathe.

Recognize and welcome God into the room.

See God in the eyes of those whose days were also tough, whose minds were also racing as they came, whose problems are weighing them down—despite their attempt to mask them.

Welcome God, who is tired of being ignored at your church meetings and who wants them to be meetings where everyone is really present—including God.

O God, we did what we could and we are glad we could do it. As we go to our rest this day, let us remember how glad we are to be a part of your people. May what we do matter to the future and honor our past. Amen.

How to Use This Book

Here are several suggestions for using the prayers and devotions in this book:

- Start by lighting a candle, a sign and symbol of God's presence, and that we meet in that presence.

- If people are fidgeting and visiting, wait until you have their full attention before you begin.

- Before you share the reading invite people to be in silence for a moment or two, and to take a deep breath, that "we may become present to God and to one another."

- If time permits, you might pause after reading the devotional and before the prayer and ask, "Was there a word or phrase in this devotional that spoke to you, that struck you or jumped out at you?" People may name the word or phrase aloud. There is no need for further comment or discussion.

- Conclude with the prayer that follows the devotion. If there are particular concerns to be included in the prayer, for your church, or the world, or members of the group, add those.

Here are a few more suggestions for having a good church meeting:

- Keep a prayerful attitude during the meeting.

- Don't over-speak or under-speak.

- Listen before speaking.

- Check if you don't understand something: "Help me understand what you mean."

- Participate, don't dominate. If someone is dominating, gently ask for a review from the group, inviting participation of all.

- Begin and end on time.

- End the meeting with prayer; perhaps something like this:

  O God, we did what we could and we are glad we could do it. As we go to our rest this day, let us remember how glad we are to be a part of your people. May what we do matter to the future and honor our past. Amen.

- Plan on an ending that allows ten minutes after the final prayer for people to informally talk. "Parking lot" discussions are important ones. Act as though you expect them. Keep people connected, and on task, even after the meeting is done.

DIFFERENT GIFTS

"Having gifts
that differ
according to
the grace given
to us, let us
use them."

Romans 12:6

Both/And in an Either/Or World

Anthony B. Robinson

SCRIPTURE

"To each is given the manifestation of the Spirit for the common good."

1 Corinthians 12: 4-17

REFLECTION

Every now and again someone says, "If only we were like the early church, when everyone was full of faith and lived in total harmony." I suggest reading the New Testament's letters about actual early churches. Paul's to the Corinthians will do. He wrote to a quarreling, contentious congregation. Paul cautioned against spiritual arrogance, suggesting to those who thought of themselves as the enlightened that though "knowledge puffs up, love builds up."

Paul affirmed a two-sided truth: individual gifts and their expression are really important and the life of the group, the community or congregation, is really important, too. It's not either the sacred individual or the sacred community; it's both/and. In writing, "To each is given the manifestation of the Spirit," Paul affirmed that each and every person in the congregation is given a gift of the Spirit. Amazing! No one is gift-less, unimportant or less than. In writing, "To each is given the manifestation of the Spirit for the common good," Paul reminds us that individual gifts and their expression aren't the whole point. The point is a "common good," building up the church and its witness to God.

When our kids were teenagers we affirmed a similar two-sided truth: "You are very special, unique and important; and you are part of a family." This Pentecost day ponder the amazing gifts of the Spirit to each, and invite each one to use their gift to build up the church and its common life and mission. "To each is given the manifestation of the Spirit for the common good."

PRAYER

Pour out your Spirit upon us this day, O God. Remind those who think too little of themselves of the gift you have given them; remind those who think too much of themselves of the common good all gifts are meant to serve. Amen.

Prison

Quinn G. Caldwell

SCRIPTURE

"Now all the tax collectors and sinners were coming near to listen to him. And the Pharisees and the scribes were grumbling and saying, 'This fellow welcomes sinners and eats with them.'"

Luke 15:1-7

REFLECTION

Every week when we celebrate communion, the last thing we say is, "The first time Jesus sat down to this meal, among those gathered there were one who would doubt him, one who would deny him, one who would betray him, and they would all leave him alone before that night was over—and he knew it. Still he sat down and ate with them. If he ate with them, surely he's ready to eat with us—baptized or not, confessed or not, Christian or not, sure or not, believer or not, saint or sinner or a little of both. All you have to be to eat at this table is hungry; God will do the rest. All things are ready; come and get it."

A prison chaplain told me that he had "stolen" those lines and begun using them when he celebrated communion at the prison. More than once, prisoners who had never done so before had come forward to receive communion. With tears in their eyes, they told him that they'd assumed that their crimes had made them unwelcome at the table. They'd heard others invite them, but had never believed it until the chaplain reminded them who Jesus himself used to eat with.

"This fellow welcomes sinners and eats with them"? I sure hope that's true; it's our only hope.

PRAYER

Come, God, come. Preside at every table where I will eat today, and do not turn away the sinners, for I don't want to go hungry. Amen.

Your Work Can Be Your Ministry

Lillian Daniel

SCRIPTURE

"Every time you cross my mind, I break out in exclamation of thanks to God. Each exclamation is a trigger to prayer. I find myself praying for you with a glad heart."

Philippians 1: 3-4

REFLECTION

One of the great pleasures of writing daily devotionals is hearing from readers, like Jim Cope, a full-time dentist and a part-time licensed minister. I told him I was interested in hearing about how being a dentist connects with the church, so he shared something he had written for his church newsletter:

"Over the years, the one aspect of general dentistry that I have enjoyed is caring for families. I have spent many appointments drying the tears of someone who has just lost a spouse, child, or loved one, giving comfort to someone facing surgery or diagnosed with a terminal illness, listening to someone in the midst of divorce, and laughing with someone over the 'joys of parenthood.' I cherish these parts of my day immensely, maybe even more so than the actual fixing of teeth. What most people probably never realize is that they become a real part of my life. When the day is done and I think over the encounters I have had, these people are in my thoughts and prayers."

What a beautiful reminder this is that every type of work can be a ministry. Anyone who deals with people can be a loving a pastoral presence, even someone heading toward your aching tooth with a drill!

Most of us don't look forward to going to the dentist. But the manner and attitude of the dentist can make all the difference. And let's not forget to include the dental hygienist, the receptionist, the clerk at the grocery store and the bank teller who cashed your check that morning. All of us can approach our work as our ministry.

PRAYER

Gracious God, allow me to do my work with a loving heart and a prayerful manner, so that I may be a blessing in someone's life today. Amen.

Sorry, That's Not My Gift

Anthony B. Robinson

SCRIPTURE

"Now concerning spiritual gifts, brothers and sisters, I do not want you to be uninformed."

1 Corinthians 12: 1

REFLECTION

I'm having second thoughts on spiritual gifts.

For a time now, we've been saying—I've been saying—that folks need to discern their particular gifts and be supported in exercising those gifts. We have done gift discernment inventories. We have offered gift discernment workshops.

And sometimes that's been terrific. Some people have named a gift they hadn't recognized and claimed a ministry that had their name written all over it. Hallelujah!

But sometimes this has gone sideways. As in, the dishes need to be washed. The trash wants taking out. The notes for the meeting need to be taken and distributed. Or someone has to ask people for a pledge for next year's budget.

And people say, "Sorry—not my gift."

Sometimes there's stuff that just needs to be done. Sometimes—well, really, all the time—there are mundane things that need to happen so the group, family, church, etc. can function. Someone has to show up to unlock the door. Someone has to take the food donations to the food bank. Someone has to count the offering.

Sometimes, in fact, it may even be good for us to do stuff—service—that has no glory in it, that isn't really fulfilling for us. We do it because it needs to be done. We serve, whether the task at hand is exactly our thing or not. And maybe we even forget about ourselves while we're doing it—which may, in the end, be at least part of the point of service in the first place.

PRAYER

God, grant me grace so to lose myself in service to you that I may be truly found. Amen.

Put Me In, Coach!

Lillian Daniel

S C R I P T U R E

Then I heard the voice of the Lord saying, "Whom shall I send, and who will go for us?" And I said, "Here am I; send me!"

Isaiah 6:1-8

R E F L E C T I O N

If you watch little kids playing basketball, you see a lot of different attitudes from the kids on the bench. Some of them look relieved to be there, glad for a bit of rest. Others seem anxious, wondering when they might get put in and if they are ready. And then there are the enthusiasts, the ones who seem unable to sit still on the bench, ready to spring to their toes, eagerly making eye contact until they just can't stand it, and finally they blurt out, "Put me in, Coach!" They are dying to get in the game.

Isaiah didn't want to get in the game at first, but when he finally got to the point when he was ready, he didn't say something passive to God, like "Ok, I'll go." He said something much stronger: "Send me." Saying, "Ok, I'll go," is reactive. Saying "Send me," is active. It's like saying, "Put me in, Coach!"

A lot of people will feel called to something but the most they can muster is an "Ok, I'll go, Lord." Then they sit back passively and wait for the pieces to fall into place, and when they don't, they say, "Oh well."

But to really follow your calling, you need energy and action. Once you say, "Here I am. Send me," you're on the record. You can't look back and say you didn't know what you were doing. You are like the kid on the bench who says, "Put me in, Coach." You may miss a few baskets, but at least you've got your heart in the game.

P R A Y E R

God, give me an active and passionate approach to whatever you want me to do in life. Here I am. Send me. Amen.

God's Holy Fools

Martin B. Copenhaver

SCRIPTURE

"Do you have eyes, and fail to see? Do you have ears, and fail to hear?"

Mark 8-18

REFLECTION

I have always identified with the disciples as they are depicted in Mark's gospel. Far from holy and wholly together, they are the original "Gang That Couldn't Shoot Straight," fumbling and fickle, often missing the point. In fact, the first sermon I preached after I was ordained was on this passage and I picked up on these themes. It was entitled, "God's Holy Fool," which was my description of the original disciples. Unfortunately, I didn't think about how that title would look on the board outside the church: "God's Holy Fool, Martin B. Copenhaver, preaching." Anyway, I digress (which isn't easy to do in 250 words!) . . .

In this passage, Jesus is speaking to his disciples after the multiplication of loaves and fishes. They were present when the crowds were fed. They had picked up the baskets of scraps that were left over after everyone had their fill. But when Jesus asks them to recall what happened, they simply report the facts: five loaves for five thousand people and twelve baskets of scraps. Jesus had given them a stunning glimpse of God's power and all they could see or remember was a picnic in the sun.

I wouldn't be so dim-witted. I wouldn't miss a miracle like that. But then I remember that the word miracle literally means, "sign that points to God." So, yes, I am still one of God's holy fools, because I am quite sure that I miss miracles—signs that point to God—every day.

PRAYER

Jesus, thank you that you love me and claim me as your own, even when I am being a dim-witted fool. Amen.

Very Good/ Not Perfect

Anthony B. Robinson

SCRIPTURE

"God saw everything that [God] had made, and indeed, it was very good. And there was evening and there was morning, the sixth day."

Genesis 1:31

REFLECTION

Did you ever notice what God says when God is all done creating the heavens and earth, the perch and porcupines, the golden retrievers and evening grosbeaks, and after God has blown the breath of life into a clay figure made in God's own image? God says, "Very good."

"Very good." Not "perfect."

For which we can be grateful. "Perfect" would have been like, "Don't touch a thing." "It's perfect, don't mess it up." It's complete, finished . . . perfect.

But "very good" is like, "This is cool, this is great, but not all done or finished." Which is a way of saying that there's a place for you and me and something for us to contribute here. "Very good," but not finished.

And another thing, did you notice how a day works in the Bible? A day is not from morning to evening. In the Bible it is from evening to evening, night and day make "a day." The day doesn't start when I get out of bed in the morning (this came as a blow to my ego). The day has been in progress for a long time (without me). While I was dead to the world, God was busy. Morning light invites me to join a work-in-progress.

When I got used to it, this evening to evening day was a big relief. God was in charge. Not me, not you. It doesn't all depend on us. But then, "very good" says, "You do have a part to play, a contribution to make. We need you."

Go easy into this day–it doesn't all depend on you. But go into it with joy–you have a part to play and a contribution to make, and without you it won't be the same.

PRAYER

Thanks, God, for being such a wise and good God and creating a very good world with a place for each and every one of us to make a contribution. Amen.

SERVANT LEADERS

"The greatest among you must become like the youngest, and the leader like one who serves."

Luke 22:26

Tell Us How You Really Feel

Christina Villa

SCRIPTURE

"Rabbi, look! The fig tree that you cursed has withered."

Mark 11:20-15

REFLECTION

I'm always a little surprised to find that the Jesus in the Bible is really not the same as the Jesus in hymns and or those decorative plates your grandmother had.

Take today's Scripture. Jesus curses a fig tree and makes it wither because he was hungry and the fig tree didn't have any figs on it. Not a very good example to set for the disciples. Not very pastoral.

He doesn't do this kind of thing often, but nevertheless this scripture suggests that Jesus had an actual human personality, which means he wasn't always in a good mood. Even Jesus got aggravated. And he let it show.

Jesus was perfectly good, but he wasn't always perfectly nice. One of the many reasons I would never make it as a clergy person is that people expect ministers to be not only ultra-good, but also super-nice and pastoral all the time. Not even Jesus could manage that. And I wonder: is that what we really want in our spiritual leaders?

In my earlier years of working among ministers, I spent a lot of time in meetings trying to figure out how they really felt. Anything negative was phrased so carefully that I frequently thought something was being praised when in fact it was being criticized. I remember one former colleague who would energetically nod his head up and down while saying, "No, I don't think so."

This is what happens when we forget that nice and good aren't the same thing. Let's give our pastors a break and let them have actual human personalities, just like the rest of us. And Jesus.

PRAYER

Please watch over those who serve you and care for all of us. Keep us from making unfair demands on them. Remind us that their jobs are not easy. Make us grateful for them. Amen.

So How's Your Job Going?

Ron Buford

SCRIPTURE

The people quarreled with Moses, and said, "Give us water to drink." . . . the people thirsted there for water; and the people complained against Moses and said, "Why did you bring us out of Egypt, to kill us and our children and livestock with thirst?" So Moses cried out to the Lord, "What shall I do with this people? They are almost ready to stone me."'

Exodus 17: 1-7

REFLECTION

The next time you complain about your job, think of Moses. The people said they wanted out of slavery . . . until they got out. In reality, most preferred the reality of known oppression over the greater possibilities of unknown freedom . . . and for good reason. If everyone loved the wilderness risk, who would watch the kids or punch the clock so that everyone gets fed?

Moses, people need water!

Human instinct, bred by a million years of survival, knows that running off into the wilderness can shorten one's lifespan. Harriet Tubman, conductor on the Underground Railroad, carried a shotgun for this very reason. When a slave's natural inclination to turn around arose, with shotgun cocked, she said, "Run or die." Returning slaves were almost certainly caught and tortured to compromise Underground Railroad secrecy.

Let's give God thanks for the "Moses leaders" in our society who, though as afraid as the rest of us, mask it well. Leaders who face the wilderness challenges and the people continually asking, "Are we there yet?" Leaders who face betrayal by their closest allies because it's easier to convince people to turn around and go back.

You know these Moses leaders; there are a few of them everywhere: in government, churches, and companies; in social and environmental action, and many other places. Pray for them. It costs them and those who love them a lot to believe the world can change. And as you pray for them, remember Moses crying to the Lord, "What shall I do with this people?"

PRAYER

Gracious God, thank you for leaders who risk and those who don't; together they give us balance. Give them all strength to lead with integrity and perseverance. Please speak to their hearts and give them hearts for the people, despite the abuse we give them. Amen.

Followership

Anthony B. Robinson

SCRIPTURE

"As Jesus was walking along, he saw a man called Matthew sitting at the tax booth; and he said to him, 'Follow me.' And he got up and followed him."

Matthew 9: 9

REFLECTION

If you've been to a college orientation or school tour recently, there's a pretty good chance that the college or university touted itself as being in the business of "educating tomorrow's leaders." It's difficult, however, to imagine a school that would announce we "educate tomorrow's followers."

Leadership is all the rage. What about the other side of the coin? What about followership?

Unitarian minister Paul Beedle describes "followership" as, "The discipline of supporting leaders and helping them lead well. It is not submission, but the wise and good care of leaders, done out of a sense of gratitude for their willingness to take on the responsibilities of leadership, and a sense of hope and faith in their abilities and potential."

Beedle is right. Good followership is not submission or blind loyalty. It is thoughtful and responsive. And it is also, as he says, a "discipline." Being a good follower asks something of us.

Often these days, we put such emphasis on leadership that when we get the "leader" we imagine our work is done. Then we're surprised when yet another leader fails to be "the one." Effective leadership involves a partnership of leaders and followers. It involves followers who appreciate the importance and challenge of leadership. It involves followers who are willing to manage their expectations and not insist on their own way.

Just as leadership is something we grow into and grow at, so it is with followership. Jesus' followers, the disciples, weren't always all that good at it. But they kept at it and before long it was their turn to be leaders.

PRAYER

We thank you, God, for those who have accepted the task and challenge of leadership in our church. Teach us to be good, wise and mature followers to your glory. Amen.

Awesome

Quinn G. Caldwell

SCRIPTURE

" . . . because you arose,
Deborah, arose as
a mother in Israel."

Judges 5:7

REFLECTION

Those who have trouble with women's leadership in religious institutions (or political ones, for that matter) could use to spend a little time with Deborah. She's awesome: the most powerful prophet of her day (read: she knew what God was saying), she was also its judge (read: everybody did what she said). They called her the mother of the nation. She was such a force that Barak, the best general in Israel, would refuse to go into battle without her by his side. The story says that through her leadership, God gave the Israelites victory over their enemies, and peace for 40 years. All this in what was definitely a man's world. Like I said, awesome.

Today's passage is part of a song of victory that Deborah and Barak sing together; the excerpt is from a part that Barak sings to the people about Deborah's greatness.

What particular gifts of leadership do the women in your church bring? Who are the judges, the generals, the mothers, and the prophetesses that shape your congregation's life? When was the last time you sang a song—public or otherwise—of their greatness?

PRAYER

Gracious and loving God, we give thanks for all the gifts of women's leadership in our churches, in all their forms. Grant us the grace to see and celebrate and be blessed by these gifts wherever you have given them, for your sake and for ours. Amen.

Glimpses of the Future

Martin B.
Copenhaver

S C R I P T U R E

"I commend to you our sister Phoebe, a deacon of the church at Cenchreae, so that you may welcome her in the Lord as is fitting for the saints, and help her in whatever she may require from you."

Romans 16:1-2

R E F L E C T I O N

Sometimes we can glimpse the future through an individual. In some people, the future seems to arrive ahead of schedule.

In some of his letters, the Apostle Paul limited the role of women in the church. For instance, he wrote that women should be silent in church (which, you have to admit, is pretty limiting). But here, as Paul writes to the Romans, he commends a woman named Phoebe to them. She will soon be traveling to Rome, and Paul wants to make sure that she is properly received. He uses the title "deacon" (some translations render her title as "minister") in recognition of her authority. He then admonishes the members of the Roman church to do whatever she might need or ask. Whatever Paul may have thought of women's role in the church in general, in Phoebe he caught a glimpse of the future.

When my grandmother was fourteen years old, in the late 1800s, she told her Presbyterian minister that she felt called to the ministry. He informed her that she must be mistaken because God doesn't call women into the ministry. So my grandmother went in search of a denomination that would ordain her. She was ordained in 1902 in the Christian Church, a predecessor denomination of the United Church of Christ. As a United Church of Christ pastor, I am proud that our church consistently seems to be able to catch early glimpses of the future.

P R A Y E R

Dear God, keep us open to the glimpses of the future, your future, that we see around us this day. Amen.

More Power to You

Anthony B. Robinson

SCRIPTURE

"The voice of the Lord flashes forth flames of fire. The voice of the Lord shakes the wilderness."

Psalm 29:7-8

REFLECTION

In her wonderful book *Nurturing Spiritual Depth in Christian Worship,* Janice Jean Springer writes, "Worship can be—and I would say it should be—about power. It is about God's power. It is about how we can access that power for our lives, for service to others, for our justice-making."

If you don't believe Janice check out Psalm 29. God is powerful. God's word is powerful. It "flashes forth flames of fire."

And in the New Testament, Paul says that the gospel isn't just words; it is power, a power that changes everything.

We in the church appear to be terribly ambivalent about power. I've heard some say, "Power is bad." We're not sure pastors should have power or exercise it. We create denominational leadership positions shorn of power. We aren't quite sure if we want to experience God's power in worship—especially if it challenges our power.

There are good reasons for this. Power has often been misused or abused. But rightful concern about power's abuse may blind us to another serious problem—what happens when legitimate power is absent, not exercised for the good of the church or is undermined. Then there's a power vacuum, and churches—like nature—abhor a vacuum. Power-grabbers move in.

My friend Kenneth Samuel told me, "If my people don't leave church with more power than they had when they came into church, they aren't coming back to church." Worship and faith are about power, power that changes lives and changes the world.

More power to you.

PRAYER

Come Holy Spirit, break us open and make us new. Amen.

Queen for the Day

Donna Schaper

SCRIPTURE

"Every high priest chosen from among mortals is put in charge of things pertaining to God on their behalf, to offer gifts and sacrifices for sins. He is able to deal gently with the ignorant and wayward, since he himself is subject to weakness."

Hebrews 4:1-2

REFLECTION

It will come as no surprise that pastors and priests are sinners. You might want to think something else, as it is so spiritually convenient to have a spiritual surrogate. But your house will be built on sand.

It is amazing how often people project their hopes in the divine on their minister. To be a decent minister, it is crucial to avoid those projections. I only take them on one day a month. I call it Queen for the Day. On that day, I imagine I can help people manage their loneliness, their debt, and their boredom. I consent to their projections and brag about how many appointments I have. I act like I know more about God than they do. Sometimes I even offer advice, which is a sure sign that I have granted permission to the projections, sustained spiritual surrogacy, risked ridiculousness. On that day I complain especially about how busy I am, how in demand I am, how irreplaceable I am.

When the day is over, I have to go back to the truth. Even the highest priest had to face her maker, his God, their inadequacy to carry the spiritual weight that is only managed by shoulders that share it. I prefer the normal day to the special day, as do most Queens. It has more truth in it.

PRAYER

O God, who made not one of us perfect, grant us the reach towards grace anyway. Give us that perfect humility that allows us to wake up each day and come towards you with strong shoulders. Give us shoulders that know the limits of what they can bear and wisely seek partners to make the load easy and the burden light. Amen.

A Messy Desk

Martin B.
Copenhaver

SCRIPTURE

"All have sinned and fall short
of the glory of God."

Romans 3:23

REFLECTION

I have always had a messy desk. I used to claim that it was actually more efficient not to spend all of that time filing things away. I even seemed to take pride in surveying the mountain ranges of papers on my desk and somehow being able to pull out just the right one. I dubbed my desk a "wilderness of free association."

Every once in a while I would put everything away, which was never a permanent solution, but more like pruning to allow for further growth.

But, to be honest, I have always felt self-conscious about my messy desk. All of my colleagues have tidy desks. If their desks were beds they would have hospital corners.

Then one day a parishioner came into my office, looked at my messy desk and said, "Martin, you've got to get it together! If you can't hold it together what is the hope for the rest of us?"

Ever since she said that I have made a point of not cleaning my desk. The mess is a reminder to me, and to anyone who comes into my office, that I don't have it together and that, indeed, none of us does. And a messy desk is the least of it. Our lives, in various ways and to varying degrees, are not tidy or properly ordered. "All have sinned and fall short of the glory of God," is the way Paul put it.

So I no longer claim that my messy desk is more efficient. I don't call it a wilderness of free association. Now I think of it as a call to confession.

PRAYER

God, let's look together at the mess and if, for whatever reason, I cannot clean it up, hear my prayer of confession . . . Amen.

Not "Staff"

Anthony B. Robinson

SCRIPTURE

"If I proclaim the gospel, this gives me no ground for boasting, for an obligation is laid on me, and woe to me if I do not proclaim the gospel."

1 Corinthians 9:16

REFLECTION

A few years back I got grumpy about hearing myself, as an ordained minister, referred to as "staff," as in "our church staff." In a way, of course, it was true. My colleagues and I were "church staff." But in another way it seemed to me misleading and a bad sign.

It's not that I have illusions that clergy are better or more spiritual than others in the church. For a fact I know we're not. Calling ministers "staff" made it sound like we were nothing more than employees of the congregation.

Here in today's passage from Paul's letter to the church in Corinth, Paul concludes a long discussion about whether preachers should be paid or not (he says they should) by saying that he doesn't do this work just because it's a job. He does it because God has called him. Somehow, he just has to do it. He can't not do it. He is under obligation to God and to the gospel. When I am true to myself, that's how it is for me. I don't preach the gospel because I am a pastor; I am a pastor because I must preach the gospel.

I struggle with the "staff" thing because I worry that what we call ordained ministers is a reflection of how we think about the church itself.

The church isn't just another social club, only with stained glass. We are something more, much more. We are The Church of Jesus Christ. The Church belongs to God and is called of God to be something grand and glorious, a witness to the resurrection and to the truth of God. Light to the world. Salt to the earth. At least sometimes the church seems in danger of morphing into a "salt substitute."

PRAYER

Deliver your church, O Lord, from wavering and fear, from sin and scandal, that we may shine as a light to the world and be as a city set on a hill. Amen.

RULES

"Now it is evident
that no one is
justified before
God by the law."

Galatians 3:11

Against the Pinched

Quinn G. Caldwell

SCRIPTURE

"...a woman came to him with an alabaster jar of very costly ointment, and she poured it on his head as he sat at the table. But when the disciples saw it, they were angry and said, 'Why this waste? For this ointment could have been sold for a large sum, and the money given to the poor.'"

Matthew 26: 7-9

REFLECTION

OK, so the disciples were obviously right here. They'd been listening to Jesus, and they knew what the faithful do with rich things: sell them and give them to the poor. Jesus had said as much, to the rich young man who'd asked him how to get eternal life. They were only following what he'd told them.

On the other hand, they were using his words as a weapon—and that just never sits well with Jesus. When the letter of the law gets in the way of the Spirit of praise, when the rules are used to elevate oneself over others, when those who love God so much they can't help it get beaten down by those who are and must always be "right," Jesus gets mad. Against the pinched and petty, against the always-prudent, against those whose following of commandments gets in the way of their devotion to God, Matthew tells this story of spontaneous and unseemly devotion.

Today, find a way to loosen up, let go, and worship God as the unnamed woman did. Do something unexpected: skip across the room for joy, write a big check to a charity, sing a nonsense song of praise, dance around like a fool for God. Be spontaneous, unseemly, even wasteful in your worship, and for once, don't worry about what the rest of us think.

PRAYER

God, help me to live a life of praise, open to you and unpinched by judgment. Amen.

The Rules Were Followed

Lillian Daniel

S C R I P T U R E

"But the leader of the synagogue, indignant because Jesus had cured on the sabbath, kept saying to the crowd, 'There are six days on which work ought to be done; come on those days and be cured, and not on the sabbath day.' But the Lord answered him and said, 'You hypocrites!'"

Luke 13:14-15

R E F L E C T I O N

My neighbor invited my daughter and me to go with her to try out a class at the new gym in town. When we stopped at the front desk to check in, the lady at the counter discovered that my neighbor had brought her daughter's membership card instead of her own. That took a few minutes to work out. Then she realized that we were guests and brought out multiple forms for us to fill out. OK, I can understand there is paper work. But then she charged us $10 each and we had no cash. By now the class had started.

After paying by credit card, we made the mistake of grumbling that by now the class was half over. "Oh, you didn't tell me you were trying out a class," she said. "That will be another $6!"

At that point my daughter did the math and realized that we were about to spend $32 for a day, when a three-month trial membership was $90. "Can we take the class and then just sign up for that instead?" The lady at the counter looked at us like we were insane. No, we had to join as members first. After ripping up the old forms and filling out all those new forms, she concluded, "Everything's official and now you can go to the class just as long as you have copies of your birth certificates."

By then the class was over, our tempers were hot and I felt like an absolute idiot for wasting all that time. I don't ever want to see that gym again. But here's the good news. All the rules had been followed.

P R A Y E R

Jesus, you broke the rules to reach out to other people. Guide us when people and relationships are more important than rules. And thank you for welcoming us wherever we are on life's journey, regardless of birth certificates, fees or paperwork. Amen.

Law

Quinn G. Caldwell

SCRIPTURE

"Now it is evident that no one is justified before God by the law."

Galatians 3:11

REFLECTION

"Do we need to circumcise the kids?" Circumcision was prescribed by the Jewish Law. The question in Galatia was whether the Gentiles who had come to follow Jesus needed to follow the Law as well. Paul's answer? No. The Jews should continue following Jesus as Jews, which meant obeying the Law. The Gentiles, on the other hand, should follow Jesus as Gentiles, without the Law. Both groups should respect the others, and remember what joined them.

Are there good laws of living which you follow that others in your church don't? If you wear a knee-length skirt every Sunday, can you live with the one who shows up in short shorts, since she loves Jesus as much as you do? If you worship God by treating your body like a temple, can you live with the junk-food eating smoker, since he's trying in his own ways to please God? What about your rules about tattoos, or breastfeeding in public, or loud children in church, or cohabitation before marriage, or praise music in church or whatever else? On how many of them must we all agree, and on how many can we have the kind of diversity that makes the God who loves both Jews and Gentiles smile?

PRAYER

God, when a rule I follow for you sake is essential, grant that I may stick to it and stick up for it. When it isn't, show me and give me the grace to live with those who make a different choice. Amen.

GROUP DYNAMICS

"... admonish
the idlers,
encourage the
fainthearted,
help the weak,
be patient with
all of them."

1 Thesssalonians 5:14

Rabble

Quinn G. Caldwell

SCRIPTURE

"The rabble among them had a strong craving; and the Israelites also wept again, and said, 'If only we had meat to eat!'"

Numbers 11:4

REFLECTION

Those who lead groups of people, or who spend time in groups of people, know how just one person can have a huge impact on a gathering: Committee chairs know that a well-placed comment can change the course of a meeting for good or ill. Hosts know that a single party pooper or high-spirited guest can break or make an event. Any minister worth her salt has mastered the tricks of raising or lowering the energy in a room full of worshipers through voice and presence and, sometimes, sheer force of will.

In today's passage, the Israelites have begun their wanderings in the desert. God has provided them with manna, both delicious and nutritious. Apparently rather boring, though, at least for some. Some "rabble" begin to complain; soon everyone has joined in and the whole thing goes kaflooey. Before it's all over, God and Moses are snapping at each other, a whole new administrative system has to be set up, great piles of quails get slaughtered, and a plague sweeps through the camp. All because of those first complainers. A few bad apples…

What groups of people will you be a part of today? Will your presence make the party, or break it, build it up or tear it down? What kind of group member will you choose to be?

PRAYER

God, guide me in every group in which I find myself today, and make me a force for the building up of your people wherever I gather with them. Amen.

Bunch Ball

Anthony B.
Robinson

S C R I P T U R E

**"Indeed, the body does
not consist of one
member but of many."**

1 Corinthians 12: 12

REFLECTION

When I coached six- and seven-year-olds in soccer, I
noticed their default style of play was "bunch ball."
Everyone ran to the ball, forming a swirling scrum
where shins were kicked, kids wailed and the ball went
nowhere. When the ball did squirt out of the pack, there
was no one there to get it.

My mantra as a soccer coach became, "Play your
position," which is not as easy as it sounds. It means
you have to know what your role is and you have to
trust your teammates to know their position and play it.
That means not rushing into someone else's part of the
field just because the ball goes there. When kids on a
soccer team got this, it had the quality of a revelation.

In many congregations we also play bunch ball. We
seem to think that everyone needs to be in on every
decision and everyone has to have the chance to express
their opinion on every matter, often second-guessing
those to whom a task or decision has been assigned.
We sanction our congregational bunch ball with words
like "participatory," "congregational" and "inclusive."

Paul spoke of the church as a body, the Body of Christ,
and suggested that the different parts (people) had
different roles. When we forget that, the body gets sick.
He urged people to play their part and respect others,
allowing them to play theirs.

Play your position. Avoid congregational bunch ball.
Trust others to play their part. Because, after all, when
we're caught in the congregational scrum, we tend to
lose sight of the goal: being part of God's mission of
saving lives and repairing a broken world.

PRAYER

**When I am tempted to rush into someone else's part of the
field and take over, help me play my position, that your
mission may be served and that you, Jesus, may be glorified.
Amen.**

Please Advise

Lillian Daniel

SCRIPTURE

"The way of fools seems right to them, but the wise listen to advice."
Proverbs 12:15

REFLECTION

Agatha Christie once said, "Good advice is to be ignored, but that's no reason not to give it."

Oscar Wilde said, "The only thing to do with good advice is to pass it on. It is never of any use to oneself."

But the book of Proverbs values advice, not so much the giving of it, but the listening to it. Wise people listen to others. That's a countercultural message in a "just follow your heart" world. But it's a message worth taking seriously.

I seldom do something foolish on purpose. I always think it is a good idea at the time. I listen to my own excellent advice and then I take it. Full steam ahead.

But if I am honest, when I look back on my mistakes, I can see that I was not eager for advice from other people. Most of my worst ideas are ideas I decided not to run by anyone else.

Fools don't intend to be foolish. But they may set themselves up to be foolish, by refusing to run a plan by another person. Sometimes the wisest thing we can do is admit that we don't possess all the wisdom. God put us here on earth to help each other. Is there someone out there with a wise word for you?

PRAYER

God, let me a conduit of your wisdom and a hearer of your word, not for my own sake but for yours. Amen.

Salty Language

Martin B. Copenhaver

SCRIPTURE

"Let your speech always be gracious, seasoned with salt."

Colossians 4:6

REFLECTION

Words matter. Words can either inspire or discourage, heal or hurt, offer a blessing or a curse. As someone once told me, "Whoever said, 'Sticks and stones can break my bones, but words can never hurt me,' must have lived among deaf mutes." As it says in Proverbs, "Rash words are like sword thrusts, but the tongue of the wise brings healing" (12:18).

So the Apostle Paul counsels us to mind our tongues, to act as if words matter: "Let your speech always be gracious, seasoned with salt." He is not advocating "salty language" in the way we use the term. In the Bible salt means many things. It preserves food, keeping it pure. Salt also is treasured as a source of healing. So Paul wants us to tend to our words as if they have that kind of power.

When I served First Congregational Church in Burlington, Vermont, one of my colleagues was Thelma Norton, a great saint of the church. In her role as Parish Visitor she had intimate access to the lives of hundreds of people and yet I never heard her speak ill of a single person. When, in the course of conversation, she came even close to speaking a harsh or judgmental word, she would stop herself and say, "Well, I'll just say Amen to that," and then move on. Her speech was always gracious in a way that inspires me still. Her language was salted in the way Paul had in mind. She was the kind of "salt of the earth" whom Jesus praised.

PRAYER

Dear God, help me to tend to my words as if they matter. Because they do. Amen.

DECISIONS

"And when you turn to the right or when you turn to the left, your ears shall hear a word behind you, saying, 'This is the way; walk in it.'"

Isaiah 30:21

A New Thing

Quinn G. Caldwell

S C R I P T U R E

"Now those who were scattered because of the persecution that took place over Stephen traveled as far as Phoenicia, Cyprus, and Antioch, and they spoke the word to no one except Jews. But among them were some men . . . who . . . spoke to the Greeks also, proclaiming the Lord Jesus."

Acts 11:19-20

REFLECTION

So here's what happened. The Apostle Stephen had been preaching in Jerusalem. As good Christian preaching sometimes will, his sermon angered his audience. They stoned him, and that understandably scared many of the other apostles out of town.

Not being timid people, they kept on preaching. And since they were Jews talking about the impact of the Jewish Jesus on the Jewish faith, they naturally talked about their faith only with other Jews. This was a sensible course of action—in theory. Problem was, it actually didn't work very well.

But then some of them started doing a new thing nobody had really thought of before: talking to the Greeks, the non-Jews. The story says that it worked so well that apostles came running from all over the Mediterranean to check it out.

There was nothing wrong with the apostles' first instinct; it just happened not to work very well, and a new thing was called for. Is there a place among the apostles you know, in your church, where a new thing is called for? Is there a way of doing things that made sense at the time, but just isn't working so well, but that you keep on doing that way anyway? And if so, what are you going to do about it?

PRAYER

God, give me the courage and vision to do a new thing for your sake when the old things stop working. Amen.

Should I Stay or Should I Go?

Anthony B. Robinson

SCRIPTURE

"Stay in the city until you have been clothed with power from on high."

Luke 24: 49

REFLECTION

The Gospels of Matthew and Luke conclude in quite different ways. In Matthew the disciples are told, "Go and make disciples." "Go." In Luke, they are told to "Stay," sit tight, wait in Jerusalem, stay put until you are clothed with power from on high. I don't imagine that the band, the Clash, had the New Testament in mind when they sang, "Should I Stay or Should I Go?" but they could have.

Generally, I am more of a Matthew type than a Luke type. I prefer to go, to get on with it, to move, to do and to act. But there is a time for waiting. Waiting until the time is right. Waiting until some gift of power and grace, not our own, comes upon us to make it possible for us to do what cannot be done in our own strength alone.

"Stay" said Luke, wait. But it's not just waiting. It's waiting for the Spirit, for a power not our own to come upon us, to clothe us. There are things that need doing in this world that are beyond our ability to accomplish solely by our own effort. God's word, God's incursion, God's Spirit are required. "Stay in the city until you have been clothed with power from on high."

PRAYER

Veni Sancte Spiritus, Come Holy Spirit, come. Teach me to wait and to pray. To wait for you, to call upon you, to be clothed by your power from on high. Amen.

What's to Become of the Double-Minded?

Martin B.
Copenhaver

SCRIPTURE

"I hate the double-minded."

Psalm 119

REFLECTION

"I am of two minds on that," we often say in a situation that is difficult to assess or when the correct course of action is not yet clear. So we respond to the words of the poet Robert Frost in his famous poem, "The Road Not Taken":

Two roads diverged in a yellow wood,

And sorry I could not travel both . . .

We admire people who pause at a fork in the road. Often they are the ones who are able to see both sides of an issue, and they know how to weigh options.

So why does the writer of this psalm envision God saying, "I hate the double-minded"? What's so wrong with being of two minds?

Nothing is wrong with being double-minded in the time before making a decision. But, sooner or later, commitment is called for. You cannot plow a field by turning it over in your mind. Eventually it comes time to act. As novelist Albert Camus observed, sometimes we must make a 100 percent commitment to something about which we are only 51 percent certain.

The perpetually double-minded never get very far from home because they get stuck at the first fork in the road. For them—for all of us, at one time or another—it is best to heed the advice of Yogi Berra: "When you get to a fork in the road, take it."

PRAYER

O God, meet me at the crossroads. Show me the way I am to go. Then give me the courage to act. Amen.

Look Up, I Can Help

Anthony B. Robinson

SCRIPTURE

"Hope in the Lord! Be strong! Let your heart take courage! Hope in the Lord!" Psalm 27: 14

REFLECTION

A friend shared this story about her mother who was a choir director and music teacher for her entire professional life.

If there came a time in a performance when things started to go awry—the accompanist was off-beat, or the sections were drifting from each other—the natural reaction of choir members was to hunker down, to concentrate really hard, each on his or her own music.

Usually this made things worse, as each person focused so intently on their own part they forgot to look up. "Mom," my friend said, "wanted to yell over the music, *"Just look up! I can help!"* But in the middle of the piece she just had to trust that the choir members would eventually lift their gazes of their own accord."

When things start to go awry in our own lives, we too are likely as not to hunker down. We do what we have been doing only harder. We focus on ourselves and forget to Look Up to see what is important, to regain perspective, to find guidance and strength in God.

Psalm 27 is the prayer of a person with a few things awry in their life and world. And it is a multiple-exclamation-point-reminder to "Look up!" Lift your eyes, lift your heart to the Lord. Let your heart take courage. Be strong. Look up and then put all your trust down on God.

PRAYER

So often, Holy One, I imagine it is all and only about me and my doing. Whether you are over my head or beneath my feet, I forget to look to you, to trust in you. Thank you for this ancient reminder that I can place my trust in you today. Amen.

BURNOUT

"Set all your hope
on the grace that
Jesus Christ will
bring you when he
is revealed."

1 Peter 1:13

Laboring in Vain

Anthony B.
Robinson

S C R I P T U R E

"It is too light a thing that
you should be my servant
to raise up the tribes of
Jacob and to restore the
survivors of Israel; I will
give you as a light to the
nations . . . "

Isaiah 49:6

REFLECTION

Ever feel that you have little or nothing to show for all
your hard work? Do you sometimes wonder if you have
labored in vain?

If you've known that experience, you'll find a
companion in the prophet Isaiah. God has called him
as a special servant, but now the prophet is deeply
discouraged. He prays, "I have labored in vain, I have
spent my strength for nothing and vanity . . ." (49:4).

It's hard to escape such feelings, at least at times. We
work to plan a great event, but the turnout is dismal.
We labor long and hard but when we check the numbers,
there's no confirming evidence at all. As parents we
work and sacrifice, only to hear a teenager say "I hate
you" as they slam the door.

Like Isaiah, we may sigh, "I have spent my strength for
nothing . . ."

God responds to this discouraged servant in the
strangest of ways. God gives Isaiah a new and much
bigger job. "I will give you as a light to the nations."
What could be bigger than "light to the nations"?

Isaiah feels a failure at one task and God gives him a
bigger one. What gives? Sometimes it is when our
own ideas of success go belly up that God can reach us.
Sometimes when we are tired out and ticked off from
trying to do it all—and do it all by ourselves—it is then
that God can show us a new path, a new way and a
new vision. Sometimes when we hit a wall, God opens
a door.

PRAYER

You know us, Lord; you know that we suffer times of
discouragement, times when we feel we have labored in
vain. Grant us grace to let you share the load, to let you use
us, and trust the outcomes to you. Amen.

Action Command

Donna Schaper

S C R I P T U R E

"Therefore prepare your minds for action; discipline yourselves; set all your hope on the grace that Jesus Christ will bring you when he is revealed."

1 Peter 1:13-16

REFLECTION

Action has a great public relations agency. People want to be active, not passive, engaged not distant; they remember the folk wisdom that "actions speak louder than words." But action without a prepared mind is dangerous.

Don't just stand there, we say, do something. Most of what we do when we are just "doing something" is pointless. Actions without intentions—and action without humility—can fool us into thinking we are "doing something." Such action is a short-term solution to life's long term.

Unprepared or unmindful action has become tyrannical. It is divorced from reflection, and the children, after the divorce, are suffering. Whether it is speed-up at work, emails at home, at work, on the subway, while riding a bike, or the way "we have become the tools of our tools," as Thoreau said, action is overblown. It has become something that puffs us up while exhausting us.

The old-fashioned way of talking about this dilemma is to contrast works and grace, the way our doing of even good things can conflict with our way of being grace-filled people. If you think it is all up to you and you work hard to do good, you are in danger of thinking your works have saved you and not your faith. *Sola fide,* only faith, say the old-timers. And they had no public relations agency at all.

PRAYER

O God, when action threatens to get in the way of grace, permit us conscientious objection to joining its military. Amen.

When You Feel Like Quitting

Ron Buford

SCRIPTURE

"Do you love me more than these?"

John 21:15

REFLECTION

The disciples' high hopes inspired them to drop their fishing nets and follow an odd new teacher named Jesus, who would show them a world beyond their wildest dreams. Their hopes had been dashed. Jesus had been executed. "Now what? They asked, "After Jesus, who could we love?"

Here, it is as though Peter says, "Hell, I'm going back to my old love…fishing." The others join him. Fishing all night, they catch nothing…until the resurrected Jesus mysteriously appears. And then the old magic is back. They are inundated with fish. They have breakfast with Jesus—like old times.

Jesus then teaches them one more lesson. He asks Peter, "Do you love me more than you love these fish? Don't you remember? I called you away from the safety of fishing for fish to fishing for God's dangerous dreams and dreamers on the earth. Though you feel like quitting, don't quit. Though you will surely suffer for it, don't quit. Others will get rich financially and you won't, but don't quit. Keep loving through the mystery of uncertainty to experience a sustaining abundance of Divine joy . . . just don't quit."

PRAYER

Gracious God, I want to be the person you have called me to be for today. Please help my love for you overcome doubt, discouragement, and fear. I love you more than these. Amen.

The Institution

Quinn G. Caldwell

SCRIPTURE

"Let this be recorded for a generation to come, so that a people yet unborn may praise the Lord."

Psalm 102:18

REFLECTION

Sooner or later, every churchy person gets sick of the church. They get burned out and wonder whether this is all worth it. If you ask, you will find out that the problem is not with God or faith, but with the church as an institution. It's not God, it's being asked to serve on another committee. It's being the only one that ever mows the lawn. It's too many events, too much email, too many evening meetings.

Many find themselves longing for New Testament times, back when we were a movement instead of an institution. Institutions are a pain. They take lots of work and lots of maintenance. They can suck the life out of you, fast. Movements are more fun. They are exciting, engaging, enlivening. They also tend not to last.

The reason you know anything about the faith is that once upon a time, somebody in the Jesus movement realized they needed to set up a system to pass the faith on to the future. They measured "what was worth it" not only by their own sense of fulfillment, but by their hopes for you.

I'm not saying every committee meeting the church has ever held mattered; many of them didn't. I'm saying that all institutions are annoying, *and* that the church is the one that brought your faith to you. So when you're feeling ground down by yours, right after you refuse to chair another task force, but before you decide to quit forever, just remember this: the work you're doing is at least as much for your grandkids as it is for you.

PRAYER

God, save us from committee meetings. And even when I can't see it, grant that the work I do today might introduce you to future generations tomorrow. Amen.

So Much at Stake

Martin B. Copenhaver

SCRIPTURE

"How good and pleasant it is when kindred live together in unity!"

Psalm 133

REFLECTION

Just days after Easter—the Alleluias still reverberating in the old walls of the sanctuary—some members of my congregation were embroiled in a dispute. So the Psalmist's words seem particularly timely: "How good and pleasant it is when kindred live together in unity!" We might wish that such a reminder were unnecessary in the afterglow of Easter. But if we are going to meet the Risen Christ, it is not in some otherworldly setting. No, it is going to be in a real church, in a real world, among real people who mean to love one another, but often find it difficult to do so.

I used to be fond of quoting the wag who said that the reason church fights are so fierce is that the stakes are so small. I have since concluded, however, that the observation is misleading. The occasion for church fights may be small, but the stakes are very high, indeed. Nothing short of the Realm of God is at stake in how we embody, in our everyday interactions with one another, what it means to worship the God who is love.

The church, like the family, is that rare place where we get a chance to practice living with people we did not choose. And when we love the ones we are stuck with, it is a sign and a witness to the love of God, who is stuck with us all.

PRAYER

O Risen Christ, help me to manifest the promise of Easter— the triumph of love against all odds—in my small, everyday interactions with those around me. Amen.

WHY DO WE DO THIS?

"I know your deeds, your love and faith, your service and perseverance . . ."

Revelation 2:19

Church, You're Amazing

Anthony B.
Robinson

SCRIPTURE

"I know your deeds, your love and faith, your service and perseverance, and that you are now doing more than you did at first."

Revelation 2:19

REFLECTION

These aren't easy times to be the church, are they? The financial bottom-line is nipping at your heels. Some group in the congregation is complaining of this or that. And you have to contend with headline-grabbers who attach the name of Christ and the church to their sorry, stupid schemes.

So here's a word of encouragement and appreciation for you and your church. "I know your deeds, your love and faith, your service and perseverance . . ." God is watching and God sees that you are amazing. Really.

I get to work with all sorts of congregations all across the country. I am regularly stunned. Stunned at their incredible faithfulness, at the love I see, at the acts of service and the amazing perseverance of the church and people of the church. The media are blind to this. Worse, we too are often blind to the goodness and faithfulness unfolding week by week in our own congregation.

But in every congregation I visit I see love and faith, service and perseverance. I see the poor fed, the children taught, adults seeking deeper lives, strangers welcomed, love lived and God praised. Church, you're amazing.

PRAYER

Lord, give us eyes to see the faithfulness and goodness right in our midst, and to praise you for it. Amen.

Almighty Purpose

Kenneth L. Samuel

SCRIPTURE

"Though I walk in the midst of trouble, you preserve my life; you stretch out your hand against the anger of my foes, with your right hand you save me. The Lord will fulfill his purpose for me."

Psalm 138:7-8

REFLECTION

I cannot imagine a greater living hell than that of going through life without a purpose. For me, futility is the ultimate enemy. If my pains are not connected to any greater providence; if my struggles have no meaning beyond their existential reality; if my tears are not tailored to teach me anything about a greater good, then I'd rather not take my next breath. Suffering is never easy, but it is bearable as long as we are assured that we do not suffer in vain.

Faith in God's plan or providential purpose for our lives is one thing, but the promise that nothing can block, thwart or derail that purpose ushers us into a whole new arena of faithful expectation. Our pains and pressures are all on purpose; our fears and frustrations are all on purpose; our triumphs and tragedies are all on purpose. If we connect the dots of even our darkest days, we may catch a glimpse of purposes, plans and promises that are beyond our ability to determine or fully decipher.

It's so tempting to get discouraged, and to feel that our work is all in vain. But here's the blessed assurance. God not only has a purpose for us, but God's purpose will be executed, will be completed and will be fulfilled for our good. From time to time, we all wrestle with life's inputs. But let's trust God for life's outcomes.

"Tis so sweet to trust in Jesus, Just to take him at his word.

Just to rest upon his promise, just to know 'Thus saith the Lord'

Jesus, Jesus, how I trust him, How I've proved him o'er and o'er.

Jesus, Jesus, Precious Jesus. Oh for grace to trust him more."

PRAYER

Gracious God we thank you not only for your purpose in our lives, but for the blessed assurance that despite every tribulation we face, your purpose for us will be fulfilled. Amen.

First Things First

Anthony B.
Robinson

SCRIPTURE

**"And do not keep striving for
what you are to eat and what
you are to drink, and do not
keep worrying. . . .
Instead, strive for [God's]
kingdom, and these things will
be given to you as well.
"Do not be afraid, little flock,
for it is [God's] good pleasure
to give you the kingdom."**

Luke 12:29-30

REFLECTION

I was speaking at a conference where teams from a
bunch of congregations had gathered. After a while,
someone said, "Listen, the question for us is survival.
Will our church survive? We don't have many member
No young people. Our pews are emptying out and so is
our bank account. We need you to tell us what to do to
survive."

I had to respect the pain and the earnestness. I knew the
feeling was real, and the anxiety genuine. I said, "I
understand, I do. And yet, 'How can we survive?' is the
wrong question. And I suspect that worrying it to death
isn't helping you."

"Well, what should we do?" said that worried,
good man.

"I'd suggest that you ask God to show you God's
purpose, God's calling and mission for your church.
What is God calling you to do? Call on the Lord to
show you that and give you what you need to be about
it, and leave the other things to sort themselves out.
I suspect it was something like that Jesus had in mind
when he said, "Seek first the Kingdom and these
things will be given to you as well."

There are so many congregations today worrying and
wondering if they will survive. Trust me—better, trust
Jesus. It's the wrong question. The right one is "What's
God's purpose for our church today?" Discover that and
go after it with holy love and wild abandon. Nothing
else matters.

PRAYER

**God, give us the courage to seek your will and way for us. Let
your purpose and call so take hold of us that we lose
ourselves for your sake, and thus are truly found. Amen.**

The Things That Last

Martin B. Copenhaver

S C R I P T U R E

As Jesus came out of the temple, one of his disciples said to him, "Look, Teacher, what large stones and what large buildings!" "

Mark 3:1-2

REFLECTION

In New York City you can always spot the visitors. It's not from the way they are dressed, because you can dress any way you like in New York. It isn't from their accents, because New Yorkers may have grown up in Kansas or Katmandu. Rather, the telltale sign of visitors is that they are always looking up, trying to take in the tops of the buildings.

That is how I picture the disciples as they entered Jerusalem with Jesus: "Look, Teacher, what large stones and what large buildings!"

Jesus responded, "There will not be left one stone upon another," putting the temple, in all its magnificence, into a different perspective. Like all human achievements, it was little more than a sand castle that was destined to be swept away.

We are forever confusing the lasting and the momentary. When Jesus was brought before the chief priests, he was accused of saying, "I will destroy this temple that is made with hands and in three days I will build another, not made with hands." The priests were incensed: Surely no one can destroy the temple. It will stand forever. And what is this nonsense about building a temple in three days? Any temple that could be built in three days would be felled by the first brisk wind.

But, sure enough, the temple that the priests and disciples admired no longer stands. And there was a temple built within three days of Jesus'death, and it is still standing. You are part of it—the church, a never-ending testimony to the ever-living Christ.

PRAYER

Jesus, help me not to confuse the lasting and the momentary, so that I might follow you more faithfully. Amen.

Knitting Prayer Shawls and Baby Booties

Lillian Daniel

SCRIPTURE

"For it was you who formed my inward parts; you knit me together in my mother's womb. I praise you, for I am fearfully and wonderfully made. Wonderful are your works."

Psalm 139:13-14

REFLECTION

On Tuesday nights, a group gathers in our church lobby to knit prayer shawls, baby blankets and booties for the members of our congregation. The knitting ministry meets the same night as our church council. So while we are in the conference room making big picture decisions about the life of the church, just a few feet away on the couches other people are knitting for the sick, the new babies or those in need of any kind of healing. I think it's a nice combination of ministry on Tuesday nights, like a check and balance system for what leadership in the church is all about.

I still have the prayer shawl I received from my current church when I was sick, and I still have the prayer shawl I received from my former church when my mother passed away. I went on to inherit the prayer shawl her church made for her when she first fell ill. They all lie around my house as extra blankets in the family room, ordinary objects infused with prayer in the midst of our ordinary lives.

The prayer shawl didn't cure my mother's fatal illness. But there is no question in my mind that it was a conduit of healing. It remains a symbol to me of how all our churches are knit together by the Holy Spirit.

New babies receive a hand-made gift to keep them warm, blessed by prayer before it is given away. It's a symbol of a beautiful biblical metaphor that goes back many thousands of years. It seems that people have been knitting for one another forever, perhaps ever since God, the original knitter, knit each one of us together in our mother's womb. So indeed, we are wonderfully made.

PRAYER

When I feel discouraged, unworthy or damaged, remind me that you, Divine Knitter, knit me together and made me wonderful. And when I feel cocky, superior or smug, remind me that you did the same for everyone else, too. Amen.

But God

Anthony B.
Robinson

S C R I P T U R E

"But God raised him up,
having freed him from death,
because it was impossible
for him to be held by
its power.""

Acts 2:24

R E F L E C T I O N

We sometimes overuse the little word, "but." We say
something nice to our spouse or partner as a prelude
to "but, dear . . . ." Or we express appreciation for
something said by a speaker while our words are a build
up to our "but . . . ." We discard a good idea saying, "but
I can't do that." We scatter our little negations like
weed seed.

Here, however, it's not our word of negation. It's not our
"but." It's God's.

Here in Acts, Peter has told the story of Jesus. He
repeats all the sad words again: "betrayed," "handed
over," "crucified" and "killed," each one a nail in the
coffin. The world has done its worst. But that's not the
end of the story. Peter went on, "But God." But God
has the last word. And that word is life. That word is
resurrection. "But God raised him up, having freed him
from death, because it was impossible for him to be held
by its power."

Amid the terror of the Nazi years in Germany, a leader
of the Confessing Church, Martin Niemoller, preached
a sermon titled, "But God." He spoke of all the ways
that Hitler, the Nazis, and their brutality and mendacity
seemed to have utterly triumphed. Then he said,
"But God." "But God raised him up because it was
impossible for him to be held by death's power." But
God. God will have the last word.

When it seems the end has come, "but God." When you
see no way forward or out, "but God." When death has
done its work and it seems all hope is gone, "but God."
Because of these two little words, because of the defiant
divine disjunction everything is different now.

P R A Y E R

O God, we give thanks that you have both the first word and
the last one. Trusting this, may the words we speak and the
lives we lead between be faithful to your Word. Amen.

Where is the Good Soil?

Martin B. Copenhaver

SCRIPTURE

"Seeds fell upon thorns, and the thorns grew up and choked them. Other seeds fell on good soil and brought forth grain."

Matthew 13:8

REFLECTION

The summer before I went to divinity school I attempted to act out this parable with the children and youth of a small church in rural Connecticut. Together we planted bean seeds beside the road, on the rocks, among thorns, and in fertile soil, just as the parable outlined.

In a few weeks the beans that had been planted by the side of the road, on rocks and among thorns would all have died, while the seed that had been planted in the good soil would be laden with beans. The meaning of the parable would be clear to all, and the children would skip home to sin no longer. Or so went the plan.

As the weeks passed, however, I noticed with horror that the bean planted among the thorns was keeping pace with the bean planted in the good soil. In four weeks, only one plant remained... the one among the thorns. It was doing so well that it yielded a handful of beans. The children thought this was so hilarious they planted one of the beans in a pot and gave it to me as a gift.

That summer I started out to teach one lesson and ended up learning another lesson entirely. The parable teaches that some people will be more receptive than others to what Jesus called "the word of the kingdom." But what I noticed only after attempting to act out the parable is that we cannot know where the rocks are, where the good soil is. That knowledge is given to God alone.

We simply never know where God's kingdom is going to take root. Our job is simply to spread kingdom seeds with something like abandon so they might take root where God sees fit. There is something wonderfully freeing about knowing that.

PRAYER

God, help me to spread seeds with abandon and leave to you the knowledge of where they will take root. Amen.

CONTRIBUTORS

Ron Buford former national United Church of Christ leader for the God is still speaking campaign, is enrolled at Andover Newton Theological School, Newton, Massachusetts. Ron, a participant in the *Living the Questions* series, continues to lead seminars across the nation on progressive evangelism and yes, Ron is still speaking too!

Quinn G. Caldwell is co-author of *The Unofficial Handbook of the United Church of Christ* and author of the newly released *All I Really Want: Readings for a Modern Christmas*. He lives on a small homestead in Upstate New York with his partner, their toddler, and an alarming number of animals. He is the Pastor of Plymouth Congregational Church, United Church of Christ in Syracuse, New York.

Martin B. Copenhaver has been Senior Pastor of Wellesley Village Church since 1994. He is the author of five books. His most recent book is an updated version of his first book, *Living Faith While Holding Doubts* (Pilgrim Press, 2013). Martin also writes for a number of periodicals, including *The Christian Century*, where he serves as an Editor at Large. Martin's other claim to fame is that he once made a television commercial with Larry Bird.

Lillian Daniel is the author of the best-selling *When "Spiritual But Not Religious" is Not Enough: Seeing God in Surprising Places, Even the Church.* Senior Minister of the First Congregational Church of Glen Ellyn, Illinois, her speaking engagements have taken her from Queens College, Ontario to Kings College, London.

Anthony B. Robinson is the President of the Seattle-based leadership development institute, Congregational Leadership Northwest. He is the author of a dozen books on leadership, congregational development, and the spiritual life, including the best-seller, *Transforming Congregational Culture*. He has been a featured speaker at many events and conferences across North America, most in locations you've never heard of.

Kenneth L. Samuel is the Pastor of Victory for the World Church in Stone Mountain, Georgia, and the author of *Solomon's Success: Four Essential Keys to Leadership*. He is Co-Chair of the African American Leadership Council of People for the American Way, Washington, D.C. and the proud parent of one daughter, Kendalle Marye.

Donna Schaper is the author of 32 books, most recently *Grace at Table*: *Small Spiritual Solutions to Large Material Problems,* and Senior Minister at Judson Memorial Church in New York City. She grows a superb tomato and has three children, two grandchildren and a husband whom she has known and loved for 32 years. A board member of the New York Civil Liberties Union, Schaper is an enthusiastic activist.

Christina Villa serves as a director within the national offices of the United Church of Christ, Cleveland, Ohio. She has served the UCC for more than 30 years in a variety of communications roles. Tina has two sons and a basset hound named Fred.

ALSO AVAILABLE

God is Still Speaking: 365 Daily Devotionals

A collection of devotionals for anyone who isn't interested in simple-minded inspiration or lectures, but just wants to know if God has anything to say about what they face every day.

OMG: Devotionals for Teens and Young Adults

Short reflections on confidence, reputation, gratitude, faith, listening for God, and more, by a diverse group of progressive Christian pastors from all around the U.S.

The Jesus Diaries: Who Jesus is To Me

Nine personal essays by writers with distinctive voices and diverse backgrounds that go beneath the surface to explore what Jesus really means to them.

TO ORDER, CALL 800-537-3394